ECSTASIES

I am certain of nothing but the holiness of the heart's affections and the truth of the imagination.

KEATS

JAMES

POEMS 1975–1983

* cstasies *

BROUGHTON

*Where the heart is, there the muses, there
the heart is, there the gods sojourn, and not in any geography
of fame.*

EMERSON

SYZYGY
PRESS

Ecstasies

PAINTINGS BY

GALEN GARWOOD

Paintings copyright © 1983 by Galen Garwood

First Edition

Published by Syzygy Press
~~Box 183   Mill Valley~~
~~California   94942~~

SYZYGY PRESS
P.O. BOX 1330
PORT TOWNSEND, WA 98368

Library of Congress Catalog Number: 83-061663
ISBN: 0-9608372-2-1 (paper)
ISBN: 0-9608372-3-X (cloth)

Some of the poems in this book were first
published in the following magazines: *Ark,
Atropos, The Advocate, Cinemanews, Exquisite
Corpse, Film Culture, Gay Sunshine, Io, M.,
Minotaur, New Letters, Oboe, Out Front,
River Styx, RFD, TLB Newsletter, Working Papers,
& Yellow Silk.*

Others have appeared in the following books: *To
Rexroth*, published by Ark Press; *The View from
the Top of the Mountain*, Barnwood Press; *Hymns
to Hermes, Song of the Godbody, & Odes for Odd
Occasions*, Manroot Press; *Graffiti for the Johns of
Heaven*, Syzygy Press; & *Sparks of Fire*, North
Atlantic Press.

The photograph of the bridegrooms on page 106
is by Sally Dixon.

CONTENTS

This book is for Joel
and because of him

For you   Beloved
I will open the orifices of my heart
I will empty the trashbins of my mind
I will polish the horizons of my soul

For you   Beloved
I am burning my bridges with fireworks
I am mapping improbable safaris
I am placing my demons in a rest home

For you   Beloved
I shall originate a shameless society
I shall organize a world union of lovemakers
I shall believe again in the regeneration of mankind

The

Tell me, dearest, what is love?
'Tis a lightning from above,
'Tis an arrow, 'tis a fire,
'Tis a boy they call desire.

BEAUMONT & FLETCHER

Coming

of' the

Beloved

WONDROUS THE MERGE

Had my soul tottered off to sleep
taking my potency with it?
Had they both retired before I could
leaving me a classroom somnambulist?
Why else should I at sixty-one
feel myself shriveling into fadeout?

Then on a cold seminar Monday
in walked an unannounced redeemer
disguised as a taciturn student
Brisk and resolute in scruffy mufti
he set down his backpack   shook his hair
and offered me unequivocal devotion

He dismissed my rebuffs and ultimatums
He scoffed at suggestions of disaster
He insisted he had been given authority
to provide my future happiness
Was it possible he had been sent
from some utopian headquarters?

I went to his flat to find out

✦

He had two red dogs   a yellow cat
a girl roommate   an ex boyfriend
and a bedroom ceiling covered
with blue fluorescent stars
But he was ready to renounce anything
that would not accommodate me

He said I held the key to his existence
He said he knew when he first saw me
that I was the reason for his birth
He claimed that important deities
had opened his head three times
to place my star in his brow

This is preposterous   I said
I have a wife in the suburbs
I have mortgages   children   in-laws
and a position in the community
I thoroughly sympathize   said He
Why else have I come to your rescue?

These exchanges gave me diarrhea
I tried leaving town on business
but I kept remembering the warmth
that flowed through his healing fingers
We met for lunch at Hamburger Mary's
and borrowed a bedroom for the afternoon

He brought a bouquet of blood roses
and a ruby-fat jug of red wine
He hung affections around my neck
and massaged the soles of my feet
He offered to arrange instant honeymoons
and guarantee the connecting flights

Are you mad?   I said   You are half my age
Are you frightened of your fate?   said He

◆

At Beck's Motel on the 7th of April
we went to bed for three days
disheveled the king size sheets
never changed the Do Not Disturb
ate only the fruits of discovery
drank semen and laughter and sweat

He seasoned my mouth
    sweetened my neck
    coddled my nipple
    nuzzled my belly
    groomed my groin
    buffed my buttock
    garnished my pubis
    renovated my phallus
    remodeled all my torso
until I cried out
until I cried
    I am   Yes
    I am   your Yes
      I am I am your
      Yes Yes Yes

◆

He took a studio of his own
on the windward slope of Potrero
where I spent afterschool hours
uprooting my ingrown niceties
and planting fresh beds of bliss
His sheets were grassy green

◆

In his long bathtub
he sat me opposite him
and scrubbed away my guilt

With a breakfast of sunbursts
he woke the sleeping princess
in my castle of armor

Waving blueprints of daring
for twin heroes
he roused my rusty knighthood

To the choked minstrel
aching in my throat
he proffered concerts of praise

Off the tip of his tongue
I took each tasty love word
and swallowed it whole
for my own

Are you my Book of Miracles?   I said
Are you my Bodhisattva?   said He

Ablaze in the thrust of creation
we scathed each other with verve
burned up our fears of forever
steamed ourselves deep in surrender
till I lay drenched under scorch
and joy cried out through my crown

Wondrous   Wondrous the merge
Wondrous the merge of soulmates
the surprises of recognition
Wondrous the flowerings of renewal
Wondrous the wings of the air
clapping their happy approval!

I severed my respectabilities
and bought a yellow mobile home
in an unlikely neighborhood
He moved in his toaster   his camera
and his eagerness to become
my courier   seed-carrier   and consort

Above all he brought the flying carpet
that upholsters his boundless embrace
Year after year he takes me soaring
out to the ecstacies of the cosmos
that await all beings in love

One day we shall not bother to return

THE AISLES OF EDEN

I

Do not turn away from my sickness
Despite my scars and my blisters
the festering of my heart is
   beautiful to behold

After all you caused my infection
You aroused these rampaging fevers
O beloved virus be also my cure
   Come quick to my sickbed

Cover me with healing touches
Penetrate me with panaceas
Love has given me heart trouble
   in every corner of my body

II

Was I born to worship delectability?
I eat your salad and fettucine
as if they were altar offerings

Hot from your aromatic oven
you fetch arousal into the room
like some juicy sacrifice

You tweak my nose with it
You fling it into my lap
You insist on my second helping

Were you born to cherish my eagerness?
I devour your zabaglione
as if it were the sunrise of life

III

I am into your fire
I am into your fire up to my eyes
  Hold me to the quick
  Hold me to the peak
I am into your fire head on

I am into your fire
I am into your fire with my fuel
  Heat up my smolder
  Reheat my fervor
I lay my love in your fire

I am into your fire
I am into your fire over my head
  Do me to a turn
  Burn me to the ground
I am into your fire for my life

IV

Since we are gods to one another
shall we acknowledge our sublimity?
We are as holy now as we shall ever be
I am not only consecrated by your caress
I am enshrined in my own amazement

You romp me in meadows of beatitude
You recline me on clouds of devotion
I become an erogenated grail
My chakras whirl like prayer wheels
My kundalini runneth over

This is the hilarity of holy ones
rolling out of bed in Eden
and rolling in again
We are rolling   over and over
in the aisles of Eden

THE BLISS OF WITH

I

You have come to me out of the antiquities
We have loved one another for generations
We have loved one another for centuries

You teach me to trust the voice of my voices
You teach me to believe my own believings
You touch the palpability of my possibles

Together we reflect what our mirrors conceal
Together we upgrade the sun in our meridians
We remain open night and day to transcendence

You are incompletely disguised as a mortal
You are the eternal stranger I have always known
I saw your wings this morning
                              I saw your wings

II

When you tickle my cravings
and sniff my privacies
when you douse my terror
and launch my dismemberment
I salute you in the name of
all that intimidates me
and pray for a mild winter

But you take me apart
and put me back differently
You mend my tatters
and refasten my seams
You patch my pieces
and tie my ends up
Then you totally unravel me

You have deranged my accounts
unbalanced my books
crossed my livewires
and torn up my shopping lists
I salute you in gratitude for
this devastating earthquake
You are my undoing and my altogether

III

You arouse my horizon
hurl me high into gloryhood
Never was there swifter Magnificat

Every time is always the first
Every time I am Virgin Amazed
dazed by penetrant fireflight

Surrendering to surrender
I fall into fathomless acceptance
sink into being sunk into

You explode my waterworks
submerge me in flying bliss
wash me up on the shore of paradise

My womb alas isn't copious enough
How shall I give birth to your armies
armies of ravishing redeemers?

IV

You are my coach
and my teammate
You are my coxswain
and my lifeguard
You energize the gymnasium of my bliss

Look how sportily we run our double plays
Look how we hurdle the shoddy conspiracies
that other men crawl to compete for
Look how our forward passes reach new altitudes
Aren't we ripe to relay in the happiness Olympics?

Your sinews test me
Your stamina paces me
Your arms are my emblem
your phallus my pennant
You are the front runner of the farthest heats

When we retire to fulltime shamelessness
on the all-star bench out in the pasture
may I fondle your championship tenderly
through the long afternoons   the golden afternoons
of the endless androgyne ballgames?

25

QUENCH

Quench me   Quench
I parch with desire
Thirst is my fate
thirst is my fire

I beg with my tongue
I pant with my need
for the juicy joy
of liquid seed

Drown my desert
Deliver me drench
I crave the delectable
death of quench

I desire   I thirst for
the wet of fire

I HAVE THE GOD

I have the god in my mouth

I savor the taste on my tongue
the sweet taste with the bitter

I have the god in my mouth

I relish the nip of desire
the peppery succulence

I have the god in my mouth

I sip the flavors of zest
the tang of gusto and punch

I have the god in my mouth

I feast on the spicy glory
devour the holy delicious

I swallow the god in my mouth

I sanctify in my throat
am sancitifed into my guts

I have the god   I have the god
I have the god in my mouth

ALL MY DEITIES

You came as dark marauder in the night
riding archangelic thunder
came as Adam in the dawn bloom
became Aaron in the noon heat
remained my Adonis and my Adonai

You personify every redemption
every valor in my soul's mythology
Permeating me with the numinous
you replant the heroes in my heart
and fertilize their synchronicity

Cavalier gods thrust and parry
in the tournaments of your flesh
where I clap spurs to Mercurius
where you saddle a pantheon
to the galloping of the prostate

O idolatry!   O   all my deities
idling in one immemorial combat !

KINGDOM COME

While I bask in your radiating arms
my sore coccyx and my cool buns
warm their shivers against your loins

Remember   my persistent St Christopher
how you waded across the swamp of my fear
and lifted me up to a new flight plan?

When you launched our spangled blastoff
I knew you might lead me astray
but I knew we would never go wrong

You pulled out every planetary stop
to fortify the crescendo of my pleasure
What more is there to orbit for?

All my fantasies have been fulfilled
all but my wish to be President of Oz
Oberon of San Francisco and Pope of Menutopia

Why now should I need such minor crowns
when I reign supreme in the most radiant kingdom—
the omnipotent warmth of your arms?

LEAVING THE TAJ MAHAL

Since doubtless I shall have to die
before you   my young Beloved
promise to construct for me
a transilluminated bed like this
of alabaster down and marble fleece
in an architectural amusement
where I can wait for you to rejoin me
while I watch the tourist faces
being puzzled by my smile

When at last you catch up with me
we can abandon the fancy crypt
to its envious pilgrims
and set ourselves adrift
on a flower-flowing barge
down a very holy river
burning merrily as we float away
to the niftiest eternity
that will let us in

THE ANGELS OF IGNACIO

They are the keepers of our company
keeping us in touch   keeping us in tune
They keep us widely awake to wonder
They are the keepers of our peaceful word

They can keep love from growing decrepit
keep our limbs from going rickety
keep our hotblood from thinning out
They believe in the triumph of flesh

However   beloved   one day you may find
my parts scattered like those of Orpheus
my body dismembered by vexatious women
or literal-minded literati

Do not weep when you hold my shards
Put me back together one more time
as you have done many times before
and play my organs in memory of our music

Even in my grave   even in my ashes
I shall be reconstituted by your love
thanks to our keepers   who have kept us
metamorphosing in the marvelous

Hymns

These songs are for him   and of him
my primordial redeemer
lord of my appetites and arts

to Hermes

Reveal the beautifying!
Arouse the world!

Ever through the dark night
he beguiles the tribes of mortal men

THE HOMERIC HYMN TO HERMES

HERMES MY EROS

Hermes my Eros   my shameless Titan
Lord of rejuvenating energies
Master of the rapturous in man
Tilt me and thrust   Divest and assault
Shake me with your ripe ferocity
This is my body which I shed for you

Divine tempter   immerse me in your immanence
Entice me to the service of your outrage
I touch creation when I touch your glory
I sample creation when I hold your glory
I feast on creation when I taste your glory
I shatter into song when I fill with your glory

Instruct me in the terrors of your alchemy
Regale me with the jubilance of your lust

PRIAPIC GODFATHER

Priapic godfather   befriend my plight
I am damped with maternal dreamwash
  Bend my luck
  Be my hot ruin
I bog in a sinking moonbath

Heat up my gusto   Test my fire hazard
Help me ignite my braveries
  I owe you fealty
  I beseech your fervor
Dessicate this mollycoddle swamp

Rightly I belong to your gladiators
Rightly I am champion of your heats
  Nudge my impudence
  Lend me alacrity
Let me run with the race of your wildfire

HERMES MY MASTER CHEF

My menus no longer hold water
my recipes look far-fetched
so I lay my appetites in your volatile hands
Patron of heats and heating up
master of brew and broil
can you whip up a new dish from my leftovers?

O subtle cookster
crackerjack baker
I put my trust in your transformations
Stir my bits and pieces
Turn up your piping hotness
Bake me till I turn golden and come out clean

O to be a toothsome masterpiece
an irresistible piece of resistance
O to astonish the hungers of mankind

THIS LORD

This lord   unbuttons the soul
This lord   in holy exercise
This lord   sheds dazzling tonic
This lord   with love to spare

This lord   delights in fever
This lord   defrosts cold feet
This lord   runs in high gear
This lord   with love to win

This lord   practices vigor
This lord   abounds in joy
This lord   polevaults the stars
This lord   with love so ancient
            with love so new

LORD OF THE BOYS

O Lord of the Boys   recognize your loyalists
All comrades in love are your true-born offspring
All brothers in arms are your arms-bearers

Honor our devotions   Enrich our appetites
Feed us great desires to match our hunger
that we may satisfy your desires of us

O Lord of exuberance   hero of our hopes
infect the phallic souls of all the fervent
with an epidemic faith in your potency

Then we   your henchmen   may survive to behold
      every man in his ripeness
      every partner sublime
      every odyssey exceeded
      every ecstasy excelled

HERMES MY BACCHUS

From your liquors of love I am inebriant
Hermes my Bacchus   my vintage tippler
I have drunk from the founts of your progeny

They encircle me with limbs of randy strength
bedeck me with curls from pubic nests
halo me with flowerings of penial seed

Desire has become my besotted addiction
I call all guzzlers in the vineyards of youth
to swig juicy potions from one another

What convivial quaffs   What varietal flavors
Such high cockolorum for the tastebuds

HIEROPHANT HERMES
LOVELORD OF FAITH

You are the only cure for my mortality
Who else pardons every crime in my history
and hurdles me high over thresholds?
You turn my inner nature inside out
You put me in good with the powers that be
You enlist me in the service of raunchy angels

Now that I am converted to your impudent faith
I long to beguile the rest of the world
with the seductions of your frisky gospel
until everyone believes in the holiness of sex
and all congregations surrender totally
to the arms of their own delight

What else is to be lived for
but the harvesting of love?
What else is to be loved for
but the ripening of man?

BEAR OF HEAVEN

Bear down on me   bare as a bear
with the full bearishness of heaven
Unhibernate me   Invade
Upset my stars   Uproot these trees
  Re-erupt my mountains

  Bare god of all gods
Blast an avenue to my eternities
Hurl thunderbolt from your loins
Shoot serpent into my bull's eye
Blaze the center of my desire
Burst my mind with muscular divinity
Bloom a new constellation of lovers
  over all this world

Let us be fireworking diamonds
Let us become orgasmic goldsmiths
Let us give birth to a new breed
  Lovemen of the Godbody
  Holymen of Fuckerie

HERMES BRINGER OF HEATS

Promethean member of the divine order
   you are familiar with
   our fervid privacies
   You know the measure of
   our desperate needs
Restore the world to us as once it glowed
before our captivity in the chills of guilt

   Fuse us with genital genius
   Infuse us with anal sublimity
Rekindle the purity of original sin
   Bring us fresh heats from
   the testes of the gods
to rewake the fire in our natural affections

Men are not meant to dwell in disaster
   prisoners of shame
   servants of belligerence
Men are born to love   to love and be loved
Men are the disciples of heavenly fuckerie
   Hermes   Hermes
   relight our blithe birthright

HERMES MY BUSHWACKER

Come in your swagger
closer to my target
cocksure commander of deadsure marksmen
You are the leader of
my last-ditch manhunt

With your neat knowhow
of rout and roundup
swing me over your sharpshooting shoulder
and ride me off to
the hideouts of fate

Quicken my trigger for
its biggest shootout
Set up my showdown with Bully Boy Truth
and make sure
that I die in his arms

HERMES MY SHIVA
MY DANCING LINGAM

You strike through my thighs
the shattering laser of
your double-sexed boomerang
and shiver my satoris in godsweat
Before I can recuperate
your serpents strangle
my fears of samadhi
and curdle my prana in lovemilk

You are a caution to the inhibited
cool master of Himalayan heat
Every time you rise to
dance the voracity of creation
you embody the devastating beauty
of sexual jubilance
You shudder the hidebound
and trample the child of shame

Rash destroyer   reckless begetter
stand your foothold to the end
Prance on the pruderies
Pulverize the impotent
Invite your true devotees
to dance the samsara with you
in one laughing kalpa-long orgy
before you eradicate everything

ARSONIST OF MY BODY

Arsonist of my body   He
   all that is beautiful in man
Furnace of my kingdom   He
   all that is beautiful in God
Merlin of my genitals   He
   all that is bold of touch
Firearm of my spirit   He
   all that flows into flame
Solace of my solitude   He
   O his lift and embrace
Very lion of lions   He
  O the roar
    the roar of his dance

HERMES BIRD

His Secret

This is the secret that will not stay hidden
this secret that is no secret
Such power thrives against every denial

It shimmers   It leaps   It multiplies
It glows like the waxing moon
It floods with the tides of spring

Here is the wonder of the god in man
Here is the dangling flower of Eros
This is He who awaits his ecstasy

He is too irrepressible to be polite
He is too honest to be acceptable
Such folly survives all ridicule

His fiery milk scalds the taste of love
It overflows   It proliferates
It terrifies many who label it poison

Not every man is at home with him
but he is at home with every man

This is He who believes in bliss

His Substance

He emerges from lowly beginnings
near caves and dung heaps
but his substance is divinely forged

He is in the service of the celestial
He seeds the microcosm prepared for mankind
but his miracles are taken for granted

His is the refulgent promise
His is the luminosity concealed in flesh
the starlight that heralds the rising sun

He relives the nightly copulations of the gods
and brings forth the heats of nature

He causes day to endure in the world

His Airways

His airways are immeasurable
His departure times are unscheduled
He sports reckless takeoffs to unimaginable flights

He craves transcendence
He takes wing at any altitude
Like the wind of night he launches unpredictable errands

He can ride rainbows and thunderbolts
He can lead the round-dance of the spheres
He can stand up to his waist in the bowl of the moon

Honor the slipstream of this lovebird
Approach his art with greatness of mind
or lose your wits in his soaring   in his sorcery

His Music

He rings my reaches
He wings my wording
He instructs me in
the songbook of the Sun

He fingers my edges
He sparks my wick
He teaches fire music to
all my flesh

He asks for attunement
He answers in anthems
He breathes a language that
enlightens my throat

He performs his canticle
on the pulse of my being
My soul ejaculates in
time with his heartbeat

His Volation

Holy acrobat   shaped for surprise
he rises from earth   he descends from heaven

He elevates   he glides   he plummets
he is the rise and fall of all becoming

Sacred firebird   cock of godhead
he enflames the air with his honeycomb

He is shooting star   he is divine sunstroke
he lightens all lights with his light

Melter of darkness   tourbillion of noon
his fire outburns all other fires

He thrives on resurrections
He is the phoenix of the Paraclete

He points the way   he dives for zenith
He is always prepared for paradise

It is not I, but the Other

RIMBAUD

of the Godbody

I and this mystery here we stand

WHITMAN

DANCE OF THE GODBODY

I saw the Rhythm of the World rise out of the sea
I saw the waves roll back   the sands overturn
the breathing of the tides become a swimmer dancing
I saw the Godbody come ashore on the Coast of Miwok

I had gone to the ocean in despair of the earth
despairing of the men who rule   and set the rules
men afraid to trust   afraid to risk loving
but quick to abuse   condemn   and slaughter

Then I saw the Swimming Dancer hurdle up the beach
rippling the world in the wind of his motion
The cliff   the tree   the cloud   the mountain
everything pulsed with the flow of his running

As I ran after him   trying to catch up
I bumped headon into a jiggling multitude
clods   drones   stumbling generations
all humanity fidgeting blindly in his train

On your toes! he cried   Keep in step with the cosmos!
You are all performers in the ballet of everything
and I am your choreographer for whatever move happens
I am everyone's dancing master till the end of tempo!

When he had vanished into the weather of the world
I knew then and forever how our hubbubs can harmonize
On the Coast of Miwok I had seen the Invisible Maestro
And the music of his dance keeps the singing in my days

SONG OF THE GODBODY

I breathe you   I contain you   I propel you
I am your opening and closing
I am your rising and falling
I am your thrust and surrender

I stiffen you   I melt you   I energize
I quicken your humor and heartache
I set the spark to your fluid
I stir your mixable blessing

I am your inside operator
I stretch   I sweat   I maneuver
I flex your will and your man power
I polish your launching pad

I prime your engines of quest
I fan your spontaneous combustion
I drive your vehicle of dreams
I accelerate your valor and risk

I am at the root of your folly
I am at the top of your form
In you I caper and flourish
In you I become what I am

You are my cheerful vicissitude
You are my sturdy weakness
I am your faithful bedfellow
I am your tenacious secret

I connect your links
I replenish your seeds
I bathe in your bloodstream
I bask in the raw of your nature

I am the conductor of pulse and impulse
I am the director of anatomical play
You are my theater of nervous charades
You are my circus of knack and bungle

I am your unheeded prompter
I am the slips of your tongue
I am the catch in whatever you think
I am the quirk in what you are sure of

I carry a lantern through your labyrinth
I call to you from your vitals
You hear me best when you marvel
You hear me least when you whimper

You are my ancient   You are my child
You are the brother of all your heroes
My earnest monkey   My ticklish lion
You are my zoo and my sanctum

I tune up your instruments
I play on your organs
I strum in your breast
I croon in your head

I elixirate your phallus
I enter your every orifice
I impregnate every beginning
I effervesce   I rhapsodize

You plunge into motley waters
You catch on fire when you love
You are my liquid opal
You are my burning bush

I sprout your sperm and your egg
I spawn the engodments of flesh
I shape the new body of Adam
I reshape the old body of Eve

I engender all the women of men
I generate the men of all women
I love you in every man's body
I live you in every man's lover

Trust that I know my own business
Cherish your fact and your fettle
Respect your perpetual motion
Relish your frisky divinity

You are my ripening godling
You are my fidgety angel
You are my immortal shenanigan
You are my eroding monument

I am ever your lifelong bodyguard
I am always your marathon dancer
Let your feet itch with my glory
Dance all the way to your death

CANTICLE

Open your doors   Open my windows
I dwell in you and you dwell in me
We are a duplex of comradely miracles
We are a house as large as mankind

Those we have sat lovingly beside
those we have ached for or laughed with
all those who have pierced us with joy
become residents of our habitation

Who needs to have it explained?
Who needs to have it defended?
This is an alleluia of life
This is the humming of humansong

PRAYER OF THE GODBODY

Ungrateful O sacrilegious human
why do you bind and gag my vitalities
in the haunted attic of your guilt?
Would you annihilate me with disbelief?
Do you detest your own urgency?

I am the stamina of your deliverance
I live to arouse your quintessence
Without you how could I taste a tongue
savor an armpit   relish an orgasm?
I believe in your body   Why don't you?

Do not cringe   touching me in your self
Do not flinch   rubbing against the infinite
Enjoy my finesse in your pleasures
Honor my prowess in your exploits
Together we add up to a crackerjack team

I beseech you   declare our union openly
Although my behavior may disconcert
I am the hotblood of your truth
I am the limbs of your agility
I am the arms of energetic love

CREDO OF THE GODBODY

I believe in One Body with Penis Almighty
making heaven on earth
and all things feasible and unreasonable

I believe in
  body heat
  body sweat
  body language
  body odor
and in all able bodies smooth or hairy

I believe in
  human bodies
  student bodies
  social bodies
  heavenly bodies
and all bodies that can come together

I believe in
  the nervous system
  the digestive system
  the circulatory system
  the reproductive system
and in all their activities great and small

I believe in
  the bicep
  the tricep
  the pectoral
  the lateral
and all the muscular powers of man

I believe in
  glands and groins
  bellies and balls
  titties and toes
  pudendums and prostates
and in the laying on of hands and mouths

I believe in
  the physical body
  the spiritual body
  the astral body
  the acupuncture body
and as many subtle bodies as one can get hold of

I believe in
  the Psyche
  the Kundalini
  the Id
  the Libido
and all the unnamed demons in the the mind and blood

I believe in
  the desires of the body
  the desirability of the body
  the dreams of the body
  the devotions of the body
and in all the delights that flesh is heir to

I acknowledge one orgasm for the emission of sin
and I look for the re-erections of the body
in the life of the churls to come

LITANY OF THE GODBODY

What is Godbody?   Who is he?

Godbody is the nature of every thing
        and every thing in nature
Godbody is the truth of the invisible
        and the visibility of truth

Godbody does not pick or choose
        does not interfere with instinct
        cares nothing for right and wrong
        never tells you how to behave

Godbody is every thing inside your body
        and every thing outside every body
Godbody is everything in the cosmos
        and the cosmos in every thing

Godbody never takes no for an answer
        uses every opportunity
        keeps going in spite of
        does it anywhere and often

Godbody is the great fucking interfucking
        of every fucking thing

SERMON

You on your seat there
sit up and sing out
Sing out for Eros
Love is unbelievable
so it must be believed

Believe your own loving
your passion and folly
your incredible hopes
Praise the marvels of
joy tube and love pump

If you must feel tortured
respect your misery
and be happy about it
Only the nonsensical is
at ease with the Absolute

Listen to your angels
ripening your secrets
Come to beautiful terms
with the god in your body
with the body of your god

Share flesh with others
Wake love   Make love
Clasp hearts and exuberate
And don't look back till
you are far out of sight

AVE MARIA GODBODY

Where my heart springs
out of my breast
my nipples stand erect
with love for my Lord
the Very of my life
He who fills full
the founts of my joy

My breast   my breast
it bursts with desire
to be drunk from
by all the sons of He
the sons who shall be
lovers of life and men

This my fountain   O
food for the herohood
of great fellowship
food for the Lovemen
of the Godbody
and all their progeny

CONFESSION

Even if I never arrive
   I shall keep departing
I believe in the unreachable
the unlikely and the impossible

Moses never got there
   Jesus never got there
Buddha went there but he came back
Lao-Tzu simply packed up and left

I shall not cease awaiting
   my traveler's alert
I rely upon the dimensionless
the immediate and the altogether

Imagination is
   my praise of truth
The beauty of man
is my hope and my sorrow

Wherever I may be landing
   or hoping for takeoff
I swear by affection
exuberance and clarity

The Immanence of

Angels

Does the cosmic space in which we dissolve taste of us?
Do the angels really seize nothing but what is theirs?

RILKE

BROTHERS OF THE SINGING VOID

Often my ears ring with the sound the stars make
I hear it in the songs my sky brothers sing
when they shift their voices into high unison
to praise the shining fellowship of heaven

Across the percussive silences of space
my brothers explore interstellar polyphony
and compose obstreperous oratorios
that stir old saints to dally forth in dance

Often their voices encircle the Earth
like a choral zodiac of orbiting friends
to remind me that star music is the intimate roar
of celestial bodies in orgiastic concord

Thriving on affection in their spacious glee
my harmonious brothers of the singing void
are closer to me than my own children
Soon I shall be going home to them again

DAYSTAR EXPRESS

I am an old youngster who gets up with Venus
I am an old childhood of the dawn
    I worship the morning star
    I ride the morning star
I arise early to run after my downfall

I am an old boy glowing as the light fades
I have a new childhood ready for the dusk
    I dropkick the sunrise
    I broadjump to sundown
I perish nightly on my nonstop dayshift

PAEAN FOR PAN

Brashest of the clan
my half-brother Pan is
　my pet pandemaniac
　my quite incorrigible
　my fleet unflappable
His is the pipe of my panegyric
He pantheizes my natural nature

I feed for my health on
　his organic folly
I work out on the exercise of
　his indiscretion
He is my undomesticated
my undressable beast
He is the wildlife in my bedroom

I take him for
　my cohort cavorter
　my itch-twitchy goat
　my knockout smeller
　my randy rumpus
　my pantophagous marauder

Him I adore and hump for
Him I am crazy to jump with

MORNINGS IN NEPAL

I

Journeying among the Asiatics
we searched for the local genesis
of laugh-loving fellowship
and the answer always came back in
the hands that were held
and the hearts that were buoyant

In this craggy kingdom the goatish men
wear tight pants   striped caps
and the grin of those who
prize distance but trust intimacy
Their high spirits are protected
by mountains and shamans

Nepals are northern kin to Lankas
Both loiter in chattering clusters
and lean quickly to smiling
Like the crows of their cities
they communicate raucously
in all weathers and roadways

'Good people make good country'
said the boatman at Pokhara
wigwagging his yellow oar
as he hallooed across the lake to
five chortling fishermen
washing one another's backs

II

Elevated above the everyday mountains
where they had not been seen for weeks
Machapuchare   Annapurna   the whole range
of Himalayan gods   awoke us at dawn
as they unwrapped their misty robes
and stood exposed in snowy eminence

We had come up the length of India
to pay homage to the heights of the world
Now at sunrise we knelt in dazzle
before these towering majesties
who had deigned to grant us an audience
deigned to accept our astonished tribute

Like clarions of heaven they stood trumpeting
the supremacy of their steep achievement
stirring the challenge that elevations excite
ridiculing the hope of the human leap
Throughout the morning they thundered
Endure !   Surmount !   Transcend !

How long could one bear such intimidation?
As we kept watch in hypnotized reverence
these lofty masters of the planet
slowly gathered their clouds about them
and began obliterating us from their sight
By noon they had vanished

AFTERNOONS IN CEYLON

I

Luncheon had made us hungry
   for one another
After the curry and fried bananas
we added our own heat to
   the hot afternoon
simmering in sweat and coconut oil
as our two humidities rose
   high   higher   Bang!
   outside the window
               Bang Bang!
and the houseboy's laughing shout

He had been tossing firecrackers
   at the roof
to dislodge itinerant pigeons
But at his feet had fallen
   a passing oriole
shocked into gape   beak ajar

Hurrying from the bedroom
   half-saronged
we saw him kneel to the yellow bird
fondle   cajole   kiss it   offer it
   back to the sky
Still it sat rigid in his hand

Chuckling then   you said
   Is this a golden trophy of
   our shooting match?
At which the oriole blinked
stretched and puffed
   spurted into the air
   vanished beyond the papaw tree

II

Remember
in the breeze from the lagoon
   by the surf at Trincomalee
our high pyramided tent of white
   mosquito netting
that welcomed us in to romp
transformed us into naked pirates
   pillaging intimate joy
to celebrate our liberation
from the woes of inland
   I triumphant over
buttock sore and anal ache
   you redeemed of
itches   chills   and sneeze
   both of us restored to
hearty plundering of desire
   by the surf at Trincomalee
while monkeys thumped on the tin roof
and the German couple next door
   dismembered their marriage
in the breeze from the lagoon

GOING THROUGH CUSTOMS

A Bon Voyage for Me

Before our first goodbye let me say a last hello
let my baggage declaration be an open book
I enjoy a crooked road but I like a record straight

I'm nothing very special   in my very special way
I'm a fish out of water who bathes in the sun
but I try to keep my tides on an even keel

I figure we're all aboard the same lifesize boat
Naked we shall sink   as we first came ashore
But I chuckle too much to get seasick about it

I like acrobats   wine   birdsong and puzzles
I like church bells   picnics and hot steam baths
I like my nights out and I like them tucked in bed

My dreams are more real than the fact of my sleeping
but I always go to bed with my suitcase packed
Be it earthquake or elopement   I want to be ready

Like Lucifer a bit   I'm busy loitering about
one eye on the ball and one on the goalkeeper
I'm a lazy ball of fire   catch me if you can

You won't catch commonsense sticking round me
I hate things common and I never was sensible
I post urgent letters in the trunks of trees

My penpals are unlettered demons and saints
I deal in romancement   I ecstasize man
Love is my warrior to slay the Giant Sloth

My particular sidekicks are Pan and Jesus
who are working out a world-wind pas-de-deux
We often sit laughing by old Lao-Tzu's river

My true-born parents are Hermes and Aphrodite
who gave me a new life where both ends meet
All I have to declare is the jewel in my lotus

So I'm a happy medium   a golden meanie
whose pivot may wobble but who's still on his toes
A fool and his rapture are not easily parted

Don't take me at my word if you have a wiser
Life's not a neat fit   it comes in all sizes
Wear out your own passport   wave when you're drowning
        And so be it a goodbye and bye

THE LOVERS OF THE MESSENGER

Combustible spontaneity fits our coming together
Where we connect shall accomodate our destinies
Here is a home for the other side of Fearful

We await the lost who come to their founding
We prepare the meeting of missing persons
Ours will be a message postmarked for lovers

Come into the aftermath of exhausted hatefuls
Come into the dawn of a rise in delighting
Here is an offramp to the other side of Sorrow

Love shall be heard here   or ears will die wanting
Love shall be listened to   or fears will retriumph
A wide bed must be made for warming our destinies

To bring to the fire an igniting of zeal
to bring to the fire a conflagration of wisdom
we announce the arrival   reannounce the revival

We are the lovers of the messenger

TO THE FIRE–BEARERS
OF SAGITTARIUS

This night is ruled by the high-hunting Horse-Man
Who brings his fire?   Who carries it forth?
Prometheus, stay with us   Jupiter's in charge here
Is this his firebird flying through our stars?

'We make our destinies by our choice of gods'
as Virgil knew   as we may regret
Look, I have chosen fealty to a lord of fire
Surrendering my icefloes I splash in the melting

Can we also make our gods by our choice of destinies?
Tell me what you yearn for   I can tell you who you are
Do you dream great vows?   Do you invent invocations?
Do you let your soul believe in Angelic Bowmen?

We each have an Archer who needs our recognition
We each have an Archer devoted to our needs
Stake your own claim   Shake out your arrows
Are you willing to be wed to a sacred target?

Fire-bearers, flutter not   And no wamble
Focus your insights to clarify your steed
Fly on his flame   Aim as you ride
Carry home our destinies to their radiant source!

AT THE ANDROGYNE CARNIVAL

This way   gentle men
to the Ineffable Lollapalooza
We offer you the niftiest Half & Half in captivity
Get your tickets now
See the Original Indivisible

This way   boys and boygirls
to the Ideal Impossible
Here is the Matchless Catchall alive and kicking
all twosomes imaginable
in one humdinger package

Step inside   misses and misfits
Acknowledge your symptoms
Prepare for travesties and profound transvestitures
This is the morality-shaking magician
Androgyne the Great

Behold the unseemly hermaphrodite
as he really seems
Is he the master of your questionable solutions?
Is he the mistress of
your insoluble questions?

Warning
He is addicted to effrontery
He can mess up the neatest arrangements
He can make certain that
your squirmings engulf you

He is a harmless rascal
He is a revolutionary harlot
He offers you nothing less than the risk of everything
He desires all your desires
He prickles with fecundity

Cunningest of cunts
cockadoodle of all cocks
he will dive for treasure in your deep vaginas
he will grasp your testes
and play ball with heaven

What more could you want?
What are you afraid of?
Does no one here wish to embrace the Celestial Totality?
Does no one want to live out
the whole holy story?

HERE COMES YOUR MESSIAH

Hello again   This is your overhead operator
I am the last message at the end of your line
If I plug you in   will you listen this time?

Call me Old Man Puck   Call me Peter Panic
Call me what you will but call for dear life
Are you hard of hearing when the word is deafening?

As your licentious unlicensed metaphysician
I can transplant the heart failure of your hopes
I can lift your blood pressure to ecstatic heights

Are you ready to unbutton rapture and behold insight?
Are you ready for a regimen of lubricity and laughter?
How much do you treasure your habitual agonies?

I carry no proofs of my skill or my caring
Check my credibility by my holy goosepimples
Professionally I am here to electrocute inertia

Fear not   I am the sweetest of the toughest
I have the inside track to the outer edge
I am the only sane outpatient in the theology asylum

I teach the sex of loving and the love of sexing
I preach the sacred music of the body's organs
All your governments have tried to geld me

But I am Adam with his Eve still enribbed
I am Pan with the groin of Aphrodite
I am Dionysus in the lap of the Virgin

Watch me lift the weights of joy and abandon
I jog where no propriety can walk
I am much too healthy ever to be nice

I obliterate sexual labels and categories
I annul the disastrous marriage of Either to Or
My legal name is Judge Nott the All-Embracing

In my catalog of snug-fitting anatomical parts
I include all singles and double meanings
Every imaginable union fits into my repertoire

I can't promise total victory for global endearment
Who can make the world safe for the amorous?
The universe lunches on indigestible mistakes

But I can liquidate your airtight scruples
puncture your prejudice   fumigate your dogma
I can operate on any toxic rectitude

I am Doctor Undoing   the wronghead remover
I extract the sick securities of the mind
I cure addiction to the bitter pills of guilt

I am also Polly Morphous   transorgasmic nurse
I guarantee the renewal of your rightful radiance
bright with enough glory to embarrass eternity

Come   convalesce with me in the clarity of wonder
Together we can dawdle in the hotbeds of heaven
and dance untrammeled in the palaces of wisdom

Or do you still cling to your motheaten doldrum?

The imagination can never say: was that all? for there is always more than meets the eye.

GASTON BACHELARD

The Sounds

of Vision

POEMS FOR FILMS

EROGENY

Reach
    Touch
        Discover

We are hemisheres
    ebbing and flowing
We are continents
        meeting

Discover
    my oases
        Explore me

I am
    a terrain of
    meadows and prairies
        moors   mesas
hillocks   ravines   and wild grasses
Approach
    Reach
        Touch me

Visit my archipelagos
    my tropics
        my equator
Share your shoreline
        with my peninsulas
    my coves   channels
        and deep lagoons

Graze gently
        my pastures   my pathways
Learn
        my landmarks
My topography leads to
                    uncharted regions
        savannas   sierras
        dunes   and swamps   and
                    hidden caves

I am
        an alluvial horizon
I am
        an aromatic wilderness
                of thickets
and vines and trailing branches
        mosses   and ferns
                    and herbal grottoes

I exude
        oils   attars   resin
            seedpods   pollen
        and spicy fruits

Touch
        Come near
                    Explore
this torrid geology

Out of fossil and clay
     marrow and lavaflow
our volcanic latitudes
    smolder
        swelter
our landmasses
        shift
our mudpots and fumaroles
    craters and geysers
quake
    shiver
       erupt

From tundra to jungle
from summit to riverrun
   in heatwave
     in downpour
I am
    a center of gravity
    a thermal spring
    a magnetic field
    a mercurial planet

Survey
   Savor
this succulent atlas
Cherish
    Touch
      Connect

TOGETHER

Together
        to gather
        to begin
        to come
        to be
together
        to begin to
                before
                behind
                because
                beyond
                between
                betwixt
                beside
        to be
together
        to be beside
            next to beside
            almost beside
            nearly beside
            closer beside
            alongside beside
together
        to begin
            to behold
            to befriend
            to befit
            to bestow
            to believe
            to betroth
            to belong

together

      to be   coming
      to be   he and me
      to be   me and he
      to be   he and me and we
      coming   to be
      close to be   coming

together

      to be almost   inside
      to be next to   inside
      to be nearly   inside
      to be coming   inside

together

      to be coming
         all together
         all in all together
         altogether together
         on the whole together
         wholly together
         totally together
         in toto together

together

      totally in toto wholly altogether
      all in all wholly totally on the whole

together

      altogether wholly in toto in toto
      in totally toto together altogether

together

THEY WERE LIVING THERE

They were living there
They were living there then
He was living there
He was living there
They were living there at that time

They were living there
They were living there inside
They were living there surrounded by out
They were living in
They were living out
They were living inside the outside
They were living out the inside

They were looking there
They were living there and looking
He was looking in
He was looking out
They were looking in and out
They were looking in to seeing out
They were looking into it at that time

They were looking and they were seeing
They were looking into seeing at that time
They were seeing what they looked at
They were seeing what they looked like
They were seeing eye to eye
They were liking what they saw

They were seeing the light in the wind
They were seeing the wind in the window
They were seeing the window inside and out
They were seeing the outside in the wind
They were seeing the light in the window

They were seeing the light there
They were seeing the light every day then
He was seeing the light
He was seeing the light
They were seeing the day and the night every day there
They were looking and they were seeing
They were living there in the light at that time

PROEM FOR DREAMWOOD

Somewhere there is a forest
somewhere
at the center of the world
there is a forest of the dream
a sacred wood
a grove of initiation

Somewhere there is
what there has always been:
the treasure hard to attain
the lair of the Great Goddess
the bed
of the ultimate rapture

THE GARDENER OF EDEN

I am the old dreamer who never sleeps
I am timekeeper of the timeless dance
I preserve the long rhythms of the earth
and fertilize the rounds of desire

In my evergreen arboretum
I raise flowering hopes for the world
I plant seeds of perennial affection
and wait for their passionate bloom

Would you welcome that sight if you saw it?
Revalue the view you have lost?
Could you wake to the innocent morning
and follow the risks of your heart?

Every day I grow a dream in my garden
where the beds are laid out for love
When will you come to embrace it
and join in the joy of the dance?

CALL TO DEVOTIONS

Come forth   brother souls
claim your liberty
Time for devotion
time to fraternize

Bring your orbits
into harmony
Time to plant starseed
in one another's eyes

Cavort together
in singular twos
firm in your footloose
crazy in your wise

Comrades   come forth
hurdle the taboos
Joy will be the wonder
love the surprise

SHAMAN PSALM

Listen   Brothers   Listen
The alarms are on fire
The oracles are strangled
Hear the pious vultures
condemning your existence
Hear the greedy warheads
calling for your death
Quick while there's time
Take heed   Take heart
Claim your innocence
Proclaim your fellowship
Reach to each other
Connect one another
and hold

Rescue your lifeline
Defy the destroyers
Defy the fat vandals
They call for a nation
of castrated bigots
They promise a reward
of disaster and shame
Defy them   Deny them
Quick while there's hope
Renovate man
Insist on your brotherhood
Insist on humanity
Love one another
and live

Release your mind from
the handcuffs of guilt
Take off your blinders
Focus your insight
Take off the bandages
that infect your fears
See your wounds heal when
you know your birthright
Men are not foes
Men are born loving
welcome being tingled by
the touch of devotion
Honor one another
or lose

Come   Brothers   Waken
Uproot hostility
Root out the hypocrites
Warm up your phoenix
to arouse a new era
Disarm the cutthroats
Sever the loggerheads
Offset the history
of torment and curse
Man is the species
endangered by man
Quick while there's time
Abandon your rivalries
or mourn

Deflate pugnacity
Magnify friendliness
Off with your mask
Off with your face
Dump the false guides
who travel the warpaths
Uncover your loving
Discover surrender
Rise in your essence to
the tender occasion
Unwrap your radiance
and brighten your crew
Value one another
or fall

Come forth unabashed
Come out unbuttoned
Bury belligerence
Resurrect frolic
Only through body can
you clasp the divine
Only through body can
you dance with the god
In every man's hand
the gift of compassion
In every man's hand
the beloved connection
Trust one another
or drown

Banish animosity
Summon endearment
You are kindred to
each one you greet
each one you deal with
crossing the world
Salute the love ability
in all those you meet
Elicit the beauty that
hides in all flesh
Let freedom of feeling
liberate mankind
Love one another
at last

Hold nothing back
Hold nothing in
Romp and commingle
out in the open
Parade your peculiar
Shine your monkey
Rout the sourpuss
Outrage the prig
Quick while there's room
revel in foolhardy
Keep fancies tickled
Grow fond of caress
Go forthright together
or fail

Affirm your affection
Be laughing in wisdom
You are a miracle
dismissed as a moron
You are a godbody
avoiding holiness
Claim your dimension
Insist on redemption
Love between men will
anachronize war
bring joy into office
and erogenate peace
Accept one another
and win

Relish new comrades
Freshen new dreams
Speak from the heart
Sing from the phallus
Keep holy bounce in
your intimate ballgames
Sexual fervor can
leap over galaxy
outburst the sun
football the moon
Give way to love
Give love its way
Ripen one another
or rot

Extend your vision
Stretch your exuberance
Offer your body to
the risks of delight
where soul can run naked
spirit jump high
Taste the divine on
the lips of lover
Savor the divine on
the thigh of friend
Treasure the divinity
that ignites the orgasm
Surprise the eagles
and soar

Let the weapons rust
Let the powers crumble
Open your fists
into embraces
Open your armslength
into loving circles
Be champions of hug
Be warriors of kiss
Prove in beatitude
a new breed of man
Prove that comradeship
is the crown of the gods
Cherish one another
and thrive

Listen   Brothers   Listen
The alarms are too late
This is the hour for
amorous revolt
Dare to take hold
Dare to take over
Be heroes of harmony
in bedfellow bliss
Man must love man
or war is forever
Outnumber the hawks
Outdistance the angels
Love one another
or die

This ceremony was performed on the evening of 23 July 1978
in Sausalito California on board the hundred-year-old ferryboat SS Vallejo
belonging to the Alan Watts Society for Comparative Philosophy

Behold
the

A CONNUBIAL MASQUE
FOR
JAMES & JOEL

Bridegrooms

Participants

THE GOD HERMEROS

THE PRIEST

THE BRIDEGROOMS

THE FIVE POETS

THE TWO ACOLYTES

THE WEDDING GUESTS

THE MUSICIANS

The Wedding Guests await in festive dress.
The two Acolytes come out to them
and distribute lighted tapers.
Acolyte One wears a sea-blue gown,
Acolyte Two wears a gown of flame-red.

A joyful noise: bells and gamelan.
Hermeros, spirit of the occasion, appears
wearing mainly talaria and a chiton.

HERMEROS

Dear friends of love, divest yourselves of grouch,
be intimate with cheer, be generous with caress.
For here at twilight on this venerable barge
an uncommon wedding shall be gayly solemnized.

I come to bid you welcome and to set the scene
for I am patron of such androgyne events,
being the special deity of inseparable men.
Hermeros am I called, since I was originated
by phallic Hermes in amorous sport with Eros.
Psyche and Hermaphroditus are my next of kin
so I defend impieties of the passionate
as well as improprieties of the ambivalent.
I guard the erogenous, the wise, the pulchritudinous,
and being particular friend to poets and visionaries
I come hence to put a Greekish blessing on this match.

Some cynic ones make jest of any marriage vows.
They scoff to see love's hot abandonments
tied up in bonded knots of mutual pledge.
Yet fervent oath and sacrament forever reaffirm
man's hearty lust for paradise on earth:
willingly would he enslave his life to ecstasy.

A long-destined choice of wedding will we here unfold
for these two souls have many times been betrothed,
in former lives were denied their love's desire.
Thus has their union waited centuries for this day
when we may cheer eternity's change of heart.

The music rings the bells!   Espousal rites begin!
Move forward, fellow poets, bosom friends,
to take your places for this sanctifying joy.
Follow in procession the tintinnabulating sound,
carry your tapers brightly to the altar side
and find your witnessing standpoints in the hall.

The sacral lamps are lit, the frankincense and myrrh,
the pathway of fresh petals strewn across the deck!
The gong sounds the approach!   Their coming we illuminate!
Behold the bridegrooms now!   And jubilate!

Hermeros vanishes.   The processional begins.

The Priest enters, preceded by the censing Acolytes.
The robed Poets take their places with the Guests.
Last come the Bridegrooms in gowns and garlands.

PRIEST

Dearly beloved all,
be all loved dearly here!
Love is the free play of the Divine
and we are here to bring the Divine
freely into play.

These two who stand before me
have assembled us upon this floating temple
to share in their celebration of
the deep astonishments of divine grace.
They ask to be joined sacramentally to
the enravishments of their love.

Let us praise their fine audacity.
Let us praise their risk of happiness.
Let us raise our burning lights to them
to enlighten their burning hearts!

The Guests lift their tapers high.

Let us raise our lights even higher yet
to salute the ingenuities of the gods
who prepare our profound encounters
and conduct us to our fates.

With lights thus lifted let us chant thrice
the Pleasure Mantra of the World:
Aaahhh! Aaahhh! Aaahhh!

GUESTS

Aaahhh! Aaahhh! Aaahhh!

PRIEST

Now we may lower our separate flames
and make of them one single powerful light.
Come forward, each of you in turn,
to place your candle upright in the sacred cauldron
standing at mid-center of this hall.

Let each of our lights blaze together
one unified faith in the lights of love!

> *The Guests dispose their tapers*
> *in the sand-filled bowl.*

Now the first Poet will step forth to read
the *Epithalamium* for this wedding day.

FIRST POET

Ripe in the sunfall before the moonrise
here are we gathered   here surrounded
upon the decks of art and philosophy
upon the waters and between the winds
Here are we gathered to surround two lovers
here are we witnesses to a grace of souls

Hale in the twilight before the moontime
above the fishes and beneath the birds
here are we surrounded by our faithful Guardians
gathered by our Angels of Recognition
Here are we partners to a boldness of hearts
here we gather love to surround these lovers

PRIEST

Beneath opposing forces were these souls born:
theirs is a conjunction of flame and wave,
of ember and ice, of furnace and fountain.

On this day, at the onset of Leo's yearly fire
with the moon aswim in the sea of Pisces,
we shall consummate here a significant union,
we shall unite Scorpio and Sagittarius
in a sprightly marriage of Fire and Water.

These powers who straddle the zodiac side by side
shall romp across its ecliptic in surprising harmony:
the Scorpion shall ride the Centaur through
the burning lake in the Milky Way.

Kneel now, bridegrooms both,
kneel to receive the alchemical blessing.

> *Solemn music.   The Bridegrooms kneel.*
> *Acolyte One brings from the altar*
> *one red and one blue candle.*
> *He holds the flames over the heads of*
> *the Bridegrooms.*
>
> *Acolyte Two brings a ritual vessel*
> *containing water from a Mt. Tamalpais spring*
> *and from the Pacific Ocean at Stinson Beach.*
> *With feathers from a pure white dove*
> *she sprinkles each Bridegroom three times,*
> *while tallow drips on them from the candles.*

This union triumphs in alchemical mystery.
This union transpires under the benediction of
the Divine Androgyne of All Things.

Let us hear then the Poet's *Hymn to the Androgyne.*

Praise to Androgyne   the All in One
Praise to his unbelievable truth
He loves us as we originally were
He loves us as we always are
    He is beyond the explicit
    He is the total union
    He is the transcendent single
    He is the doubles champion
He is woman man   He is goddess god
He is the seeder and the seeded
He is the Both   He is the And
He is the source and the sorcerer
    He is the her in the he
    He is the him in the she
    He is the two in the one
    He is the one beyond two
Praise to Androgyne   the Irreducible All
Praise to his unbelievable truth
He loves us as we originally were
He loves us as we always are

These holy mysteries elucidate
the great enigmas of mankind.
We all are incarnations of the Androgyne.
We all are mirrors of the Godbody.

Dearly betrothed, look now upon each other
as you repeat in unison after me
the zealous paradoxes of your love:

You are my Lover   You are my Beloved

BRIDEGROOMS

You are my Lover   You are my Beloved

PRIEST

You are my Parent   You are my Child

BRIDEGROOMS

You are my Parent   You are my Child

PRIEST

You are my Fate   You are my Soulmate

BRIDEGROOMS

You are my Fate   You are my Soulmate

PRIEST

You are my Bridegroom   You are my Bride

BRIDEGROOMS

You are my Bridegroom   You are my Bride

PRIEST

Now shall this company cheer these vows
by chanting the Pleasure Mantra three times.

GUESTS

Aaahhh! Aaahhh! Aaahhh!

PRIEST

Bring forth the grail with the communioning libation!
Bring it to the third Poet for his consecrating!

Acolyte One brings forward the ceremonial cup.

THIRD POET

This cup contains an unearthly nectar
habitually served at the weddings of wizards.
It is compounded by local seraphs and satyrs
from apricotroot   appleheart   and plumtail
poppybrine   cashewegg   and salmonbreast
larksweat   lionspray   and mothsperm
distilled in the pearly honeys of the moon.
It contains the essence of spirits in delight:
the delicious secret of the Great Intoxication.
Everyone may risk one sip.   Serve it forth!

*Acolyte One proffers the grail first
to each of the Bridegrooms.
Then he brings it to each Guest in turn
and finally back to the Priest.*

All during this communion the Third Poet
recites the Nectar Sutra *repeatedly*
until the communion concludes.

THIRD POET

Drink in remembrance of
  Adam   the Original Androgyne
  Hermes   the Passionate Shape-changer
  Krishna   the Love-spreading Flutist
  Jesus   the Bridegroom of the Godbody

Drink in remembrance of
  Shiva and his Shakti
  Rumi and his Shamsi
  Gilgamesh and his Enkidu
  David and his Jonathan

Drink in remembrance of
  Whitman and Plato
  Leonardo and Michelangelo
  Rimbaud and Cocteau
  Bach and Blake and the Bard of Avon

Drink in remembrance of all
  poets and charioteers
  philosophers and explorers
  siddhas and saints
  buddhas and bodhisattvas
and in salutation to
  all possible weddings of the gods
  on earth and in heaven

Acolyte Two brings the inlaid box
containing the wedding rings.
The Priest opens it and offers it in turn
to each of the Bridegrooms.

PRIEST

Here are the binding circlets of gold
that proclaim your treasure to one another
and proclaim your devotion before the world.

Joel, as you place the ring of wedding
on your spouse's finger
speak whatever words ring in your heart.

JOEL

Jamie   my love

At your breast I taste our troth
my mother's milk through soulsweet sweat
Centuries of eyes I've looked for yours
Beloved bearded my white haired wizard
Chiseled years reveal your beauty

Let me carry you   Let me cry
my father's come the godspilled gift
a truth I treasure in my womb
O closer my Jamie   my child newborn
Let me wrap you   anoint you with peppery secrets

Let us be hawks   and the wind our bed
will carry the Yes on its breath
My Androgyne Bride   your secrets are safe
cherished within my temple

PRIEST

James, as you place the ring of wedding
on your spouse's finger
speak whatever words ring in your heart.

JAMES

Beloved One   prize of my life
I proudly wed my soul to your flesh
You are the love I have longed for all my life
You are the love I thought I would never have in this life
You are the miracle that renews my life

My touchstone   my touchable angel
I am enfolded in your devotion
I am renewable in your rapture
You are my direct connection to the divine
You are my only and my rightful fate

I will drink love tonics from your mouth
I will absorb healing energy from your fingers
I will be nourished and renourished by your beauty
With you I will fill full   I will fulfill
I will abide till I disintegrate

PRIEST

These avowals deserve our happiest praise.
Let us repeat our Pleasure Mantra once again.

GUESTS

Aaahhh! Aaahhh! Aaahhh!

PRIEST

The Poet shall now read the Lesson for Today.

FOURTH POET

Here are the Now Commandments I give unto you.

Thou shalt   Thou shalt   And thou shalt
Thou shalt loosen   Thou shalt flow   Thou shalt flower
Thou shalt love   Thou shalt love   Thou shalt love

Thou shalt surrender the miseries of thy mind
Thou shalt retrieve the innocence of thy heart
Thou shalt relish the amazements of thy body
Thou shalt revel in thy dishevelment
Thou shalt commit ecstasies upon the earth
Thou shalt commit merriments to cheer the heavens

Thou shalt live   Thou shalt give   Thou shalt flourish
Thou shalt love   Thou shalt love   Thou shalt love
Thou shalt   Thou shalt   And thou shalt

PRIEST

Let the Lovers pledge their most intimate troth.
Let them come forth and proclaim their chakra vows.

*The Bridegrooms stand in the center of the hall
and bless with a kiss each chakra of the other,
saying in turn:*

BRIDEGROOMS

I cherish you from
the bottom of your feet to
the crown of your head.

I honor the entire temple of your body
as a holy place of infinite joy.

I bless your centers of energy
your meridians of creation
your mandalas of bliss.

I kiss now the vital centers of your torso
from your perineum to your phallus
from your navel to your heart
from your throat to your third eye.

They embrace and are uplifted.

PRIEST

In witness of these offerings of surrender
the blessing of bliss is upon all of us here.
Let us join in a *Bliss Mantra*.

FIFTH POET

Bliss   Bliss   Bliss
Bliss Us   Bliss Thus   Bliss This
Two Bliss   Both Bliss   Together Bliss
Vow Bliss   Now Bliss   Kiss Bliss
Body Bliss   Buddha Bliss   Beauty Bliss
Two-in-one Bliss   Two-in-wonder Bliss   Bliss Bliss
Bless Bliss   Bless Thus   Bless This
Bliss   Bliss   Bliss

GUESTS

Bliss!   Bliss!   Bliss!

PRIEST

Blissful Ones, be ever blessed.
Now I shall pronounce you
lovers for life   and livers for love
in all lifetimes and in all loveworlds.

BRIDEGROOMS

We thank you with our hearts and with our souls.
That you may wear our blessing as your own
we shall here encircle everyone with embrace
and with loveknots of commingled fire and water.

Fanfares. The Acolytes bring strands of colored wool.
The Bridegrooms move among the Guests and tie
two threads, one flame-red and one marine-blue,
around every neck of the assembled company.
They also bestow a kiss upon every cheek.
Hermeros reappears as an Epilogue.

HERMEROS

Our revels are not ended here, they only now begin.
Already champagne bottles blow their tops
to herald festive feasting for this night.
The largest tidbit shall be the wedding cake
with double bridegrooms in a sugared belvedere!

A wedding seems to promise delectable euphoria
while a marriage may produce vexation and dismay.
However, men like these whose love abounds in grace
possess the strength of lions and of saints
for whatever bold endeavors they may risk.

So take to heart these exaltations we have seen
and make it known that such devotions can excel.
Be fond to loving fellows and to loving fellow men
that all may rejoice as bridegrooms in the end .

He vanishes.

GUESTS

Aaahhh! Aaahhh! Aaahhh!
Bliss!   Bliss!   Bliss!

General dance.

This book is published in an edition of
2000 paperbound copies, of which 30 are
numbered 1 to 30 and signed by the
author. There are also 200 hardbound
copies, of which 26 are lettered A to Z
and signed, with an original handwritten
poem by the author.

Book Design & Calligraphy
William Stewart

Typesetting
Cass Brayton

ALSO BY JAMES BROUGHTON

BOOKS

The Playground
Musical Chairs
An Almanac for Amorists
True & False Unicorn
The Right Playmate
Tidings
High Kukus
A Long Undressing
Seeing The Light
Odes for Odd Occasions
The Androgyne Journal
Hymns to Hermes
Shaman Psalm
Graffiti for the Johns of Heaven

FILMS

Mother's Day
Four in the Afternoon
Loony Tom
The Pleasure Garden
The Bed
The Golden Positions
This is It
Dreamwood
Testament
Erogeny
Song of the Godbody
Hermes Bird
The Gardener of Eden
Devotions

James Broughton is a native Californian who has been since 1948 a luminary of the San Francisco scene for his lively achievements in poetry and filmmaking. He has produced some twenty books and as many independent films, has been the recipient of two Guggenheim Fellowships, two grants from the National Endowment for the Arts, and a Cannes Film Festival award. His principal hobby is the care and feeding of ecstasy.